Spinosaurus
The Spine

Dinosaur Books For Young Readers
By
Enrique Fiesta

Mendon Cottage Books

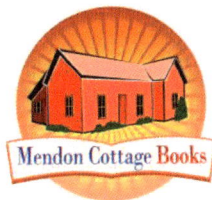

Mendon Cottage Books

JD-Biz Publishing

Read More Amazing Animal Books

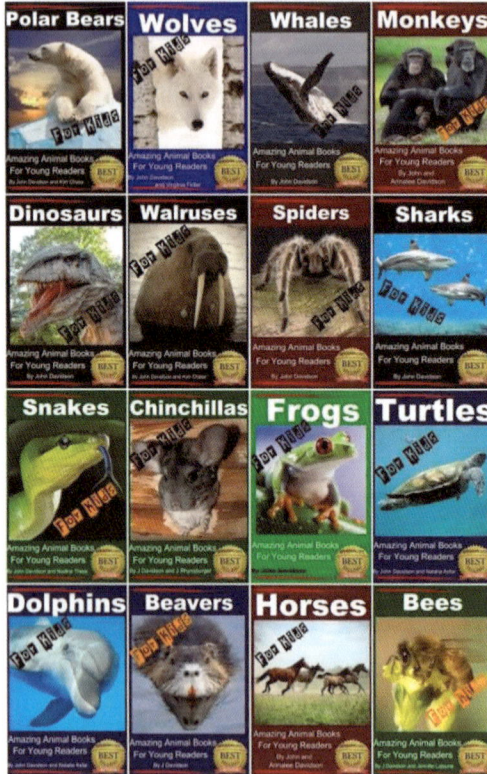

Purchase at Amazon.com

Table of Contents

Introduction

Greetings young reader! Today we are going to take a step back in time and enter the age of the dinosaurs. The dinosaurs are an extinct species of animal that began to live on the Earth over 200 million years ago. "Extinct" means that they no longer exist. The dinosaurs are some of the most intriguing and awe-inspiring animals that have existed on our planet. The dinosaurs' colossal size, strange characteristics, and mysterious disappearance make them *inherently* worthy of study and interest. Even more than these reasons, the study of dinosaurs itself is an incredible adventure which requires thought and imagination. The study of dinosaurs helps you to appreciate just how mysterious and amazing life and nature really is. Our planet supports not only us and the animals that live today, but it even supported creatures as gigantic and strange as the dinosaurs- just think how cool that is! I hope that you bring a spirit of openness and wonder to your study of the dinosaurs, and that you come to appreciate the mystery and value of the dinosaurs.

The Spinosaurus is a well-known dinosaur because of its tremendous size and the sail-like growth that protrudes from its back. The Spinosaurus was also the star of a very recent and popular dinosaur movie. We are going to discuss the strange appearance of the Spinosaurus, the behavior, and the dinosaurs that it lived with. We know what we know about the dinosaurs from a variety of sources including fossils, biology, and other scientific disciplines. Fossils are the ancient remains of the dinosaurs, the most familiar being their bones. Biological science is the study of life in general, but many scientists compare the dinosaurs to modern day animals to support their theories.

Before a talk about dinosaurs can take place it is important that we discuss the theory of evolution. Evolutionary theory supposes that all the animals we know and see today are the direct descendants of animals that existed millions of years ago. The dinosaurs and other creatures that existed millions of years ago either died out or gradually changed into different animals. For instance, birds are considered to be surviving dinosaurs because their dinosaur ancestors survived the dinosaur extinction event (we will discuss this later).

Chapter 1: Appearance

The name of the Spinosaurs is a combination of two Greek words ("spinos" and "sauros") which means "Spine Reptile." The Spinosaurus earned this name because of its distinctive and most easily recognizable trait: a series of elongated vertebrae which run down the length of the dinosaur's back. Most scientists believe that the vertebrae were connected by a thin layer of skin. The skin-covered spines would have looked similar to a Chinese fan.

There are a number of theories about the function of the sail, but the most interesting is that it was used in thermoregulation. **Thermoregulation** is the ability of an animal to control its own body temperature. If blood ran through the skin of the fan, it would have been in close contact with blowing wind. The blowing wind would have cooled the blood, and this cooled blood would have cooled the dinosaur as a whole. This affect would have made sure that dinosaur did not overheat.

Some scientists believe that the sail might have absorbed heat and warmed the dinosaur rather than cool it off. If the Spinosaurus lived in the water most of the time it is possible that it would not have been relatively cool throughout the day. The sail would have absorbed heat and as the sun warmed the blood in the sail it would have warmed the Spinosaurus. The last theory is that the spines were covered in flesh and fat, forming a large hump on the back of the Spinosaurus like a camel's hump.

The Spinosaurus was the *largest* known terrestrial predator in history. **Terrestrial** means land-dwelling and a **predator** is an animal which hunts other animals to feed. The Spinosaurus could reach a length between 41 feet to 59 feet and a weight between 7 to 23 tons. The

Spinosaurus was bigger and heavier than a school bus. The Spinosaurus belonged to a class of dinosaurs called therapods. **Therapods** are bipedal, predatory dinosaurs. The Spinosaurus was even larger than the Tyrannosaurus Rex and Giganotosaurus.

The Spinosaurus was a predator which means it was equipped with deadly claws and sharp teeth. Scientists are unsure whether or not the Spinosaurus hunted dinosaurs or fed mainly on fish. The Spinosaurus had a crocodile shaped head and jaws lined with long, sharp teeth. The fossil record suggests that the Spinosaurus fed on fish and pterosaurs depending on the season.

The Spinosaurus was covered in scales, rather than feathers like some other therapods. The color of the Spinosaurus is unknown, but it was probably colored similarly to modern crocodilians. The Spinosaurs were probably a range of colors between green, brown, and black. This is probable because the Spinosaurus is similar to modern crocodiles.

Chapter 2: Behavior

The Spinosaurus acted similarly to modern crocodilians if the fossil record proves anything. The record indicates that the Spinosaurus fed on fish, pterosaurs, and sometimes other dinosaurs. The Spinosaurus probably lived on land and in water like a crocodile.

It would have eaten fish during the more plentiful seasons and fed on pterosaurs and dinosaurs during droughts and periods when fish were scarce. We know the Spinosaurus fed mainly on fish because the Spinosaurus did not have the muscles necessary to take down powerful prey (like other dinosaurs).

The Spinosaurus could have used its sail not only for thermoregulation, but also for identification, intimidation, and mating. Spinosaurs may have been able to identify each other easily because of their prominent spines. The large size of this dinosaur combined with its tall spine would have scared away potentially dangers dinosaurs. The spine may also have been used for display purposes (like the peacock) when it was trying to attract mates. Male and female Spinosaurs may have had differently colored sails, just as many modern birds and reptiles differ in color and plumages depending on their gender.

If crocodilian behavior is any indicator of Spinosaur behavior, it is possible that the Spinosaurs were somewhat social, albeit in a disorganized manner. Unlike wolves, lions, and probably raptor species, the Spinosaurus did not hunt in a pack in order to bring down prey. The Spinosaurs probably acted like crocodiles in that if prey were taken down by a Spinosaurus others would feed on the same carcass, though after feeding the several Spinosaurs would have left each other alone.

Chapter 3: Environment

The Spinosaurus lived in Cretaceous Period Africa. The Cretaceous Period was the last period of the Mesozoic Era which was about 250 million years ago. The Mesozoic Era is split into three periods: the Triassic, Jurassic, and Cretaceous. The Cretaceous Period ended with an event that wiped out most of the dinosaurs. This dinosaur extinction event was probably caused by a combination of factors such as meteoric impact, disease, and climate change. The dinosaurs which were not able to adapt and overcome new conditions died out. The only surviving dinosaurs are modern day birds. Crocodiles and other reptiles are closely related to the dinosaurs.

The Cretaceous Period was relatively warm and the earth lacked polar ice caps. The environment inhabited by the Spinosaurus was probably a coastal region with tidal flats and channels. It probably lived in mangrove forests alongside other large predators. In these environments it would have fed on turtles, fish, and lizards. If the dinosaur were desperate, it would have hunted other dinosaurs and pterosaurs.

The Spinosaurus shared its environment with many other dinosaurs and animals; such dinosaurs include the Carcharodontosaurus, Ouranosaurus, and pterosaurs.

The Carcharodontosaurus was another extremely large therapod, and it was most likely the apex predator of Cretaceous Africa. It, too, was larger than the Tyrannosaurus Rex. The Carcharodontosaurus had teeth similar to that of the modern Great White Shark which means it could shred apart other dinosaurs with ease. The Spinosaurus and Carcharodontosaurus probably would not have hunted one another, due to the fact that they could both harm one another with their deadly teeth and claws. It is unfortunate for the Spinosaurus, though, that the Carcharodontosaurus was equipped for taking down large dinosaurs so if push came to shove the Spinosaurus would have been a potential prey item for the Carcharodontosaurus.

The Ouranosaurus is an interesting dinosaur whose name means "Valiant Reptile." It, like the Spinosaurus, possessed a large sail-like structure on its back. The Ouranosaurus was an herbivore unlike the predatory Spinosaurus. An **herbivore** is an animal who feeds on vegetation and plants to live. A submerged Spinosaurus could have surprised drinking Ouranosaurs by leaping out of water at high speeds and gripping the unsuspecting dinosaur with its jaws.

The pterosaurs were a group of flying dinosaurs that lived throughout the Mesozoic Era. The pterosaurs had leathery wings and were completely covered in scales. The pterosaurs ranged in size from about as big as a pigeon to as large as a small airplane. When pterosaurs came down to the water to drink it is highly plausible that Spinosaurs would have taken them by surprise and dragged them underwater to eat.

Conclusion

We have stepped back in time to look at this dinosaur, where and when he lived, and the dinosaurs he lived with- and what a journey it was! By using our imaginations and knowledge we can engage, wonder about, and appreciate the wonderful mystery and value of the dinosaurs. By learning about and appreciating what the dinosaurs were we come to appreciate our own present age and all the wonderful creatures that live today. We discover how varied and mysterious life really is- we look at animals today with a newfound appreciation and awe. Make sure you keep thinking, learning, and imagining, and *really* make sure that you never lose your sense of wonder.

Author Bio

Enrique Fiesta

I was born in Southwest Florida and I hold a degree in Latin and Greek language and literature. In addition to my principal studies, I have also studied philosophy, history, the natural sciences, and literature. In my spare time I devote the vast majority of my time to reading, writing, praying, and walking. I am currently pursuing legal studies in order to become an attorney. After I earn my law degree I intend to pursue a doctorate in philosophy, literature, and politics.

Our books are available at
1. Amazon.com
2. Barnes and Noble
3. Itunes
4. Kobo
5. Smashwords
6. Google Play Books

Bonus Dinosaur Content

Introduction to Dinosaurs

We will start our journey with dinosaurs with the Tyrannosaurus Rex. The fossilized remains of the Tyrannosaurus are found in the world's biggest dig sites, which are located in Montana. Palaeontologists discover new things about dinosaurs in dig sites. Dinosaurs can be huge, weird, tiny and even wonderful. The Tyrannosaurus Rex, as we will find out, was one of the huge dinosaurs palaeontologists have discovered.

Tyrannosaurus Rex

The word dinosaur is derived from the ancient Greek words "deinos" and "saurus." These words translated into English mean "terrible lizard." Dinosaurs were creatures who dwelled on Earth and dominated the life of this planet during the Mesozoic Era which was about 65 million years ago. There were also flying and marine dinosaurs and they existed with the land-dwelling dinosaurs for about 150 million years. Dinosaurs occupied every kind of environment and climate which existed on Earth at those times. They could be about as small as the size of chicken to being 100 feet long and weighing 100 tons. Dinosaurs were one of two types: one was called Ornithischia which means bird hipped, and the other Saurischia which means lizard hipped. Dinosaurs could either be herbivorous, carnivorous or omnivorous. These are long extinct animals- there are no more dinosaurs today.

Microraptor© *Michael Rosskothen - Fotolia.com*

Facts about Dinosaurs

Have you ever heard of Dinosaurs? What are they? Here are some important facts about them.

1. Dinosaurs are reptiles that lived on earth over 230 million years ago.

2. The word Dinosaur originated from Greek words "terrible lizard."

3. Dinosaurs are extinct and cannot be found on earth alive right now, but their fossils can be extracted for study.

4. The heaviest dinosaurs weighed about 80 tons, and they are called brachiosaurs. Brachiosaurs had a height of 16 meters and a length of 26 meters.

5. Dinosaurs laid eggs which can be found in many shapes and sizes. The smallest egg of a dinosaur ever found on earth is about 3 centimeters in length and a large one was about 30cm in length.

6. When dinosaur eggs become fossils they harden like rocks but maintain their structure.

7. Troodon was probably the most intelligent dinosaur. Its cranial capacity was equal to that of an average present day mammal. It had grasping hands and stereoscopic vision.

8. Ornithomiminds were the fastest dinosaurs. They were able to reach maximum speeds of 60 kilometers per hour.

Fight between Euoplocephalus tutus and Troodon formosus

9. The oldest dinosaur bones are found in Madagascar and they are around 230 million years old.

10. Micropachycephalosaurus is the longest name of a dinosaur and it means tiny thick headed lizard .It was discovered in China.

11. Thecodontosaurus Antiquus was the oldest dinosaur to be discovered in Britain .It was discovered in 1970 in a place near Bristol. It was 2.1 meters in length.

12. Up to the present over 700 species of dinosaurs have been discovered and named. Palaeontologists are carrying out more research with the aim of discovering more.

13.108 species of dinosaurs have been discovered in Britain alone.

14. Megalosaurus was the first dinosaur to be formerly named. It was named in 1824.

Dinosaur Extinction

The term extinction is used in biology to refer to the end of a species. Dinosaurs became extinct 65 million years ago at the end of the Cretaceous period. Since this took place many years ago, it is hard for scientists to find the reason that caused the dinosaurs to become extinct. Rocks and fossils are used by scientists to find out what caused the dinosaur extinction. However, there are some plausible explanations for what could have happened.

The explanations put forward include:

Volcanic eruptions
Volcanic eruption are one of the suggested reasons. According to this suggestion, there was a lot of volcanic activity that caused changes in the weather. The dinosaurs were not able to adapt to the weather changes and so they died.

Diseases
Diseases could also have caused the death of the dinosaurs. A disease could have spread rapidly and killed them.

The Ice age
The climate of the planet occasionally becomes colder. These cold-periods are called ice ages and they might have killed off the dinosaurs if they could not survive in the colder weather.

Asteroid impact

Scientists believe that a very big asteroid hit the earth during the age of the dinosaurs. An asteroid impact could have altered weather patterns and possibly lowered the temperature of the planet. This is because an asteroid impact would have ejected tons of dust particles into the sky which would have blocked sunlight. If the sun is blocked plants cannot survive, then herbivores cannot survive, and then carnivores cannot survive.

Combined reasons or Gradual extinction
It is possible that no one factor alone was responsible for the death of the dinosaurs, but possibly a combination of volcanic eruptions, asteroid collisions, and outbreak of disease.

Dinosaur Fossils

Dinosaurs are animals that existed thousands of years ago. They are of different sizes and colors. Some have wings and other appear in their own physical appearance. Dinosaur fossils have been found all over the world.

Dinosaur Fossil

Fossils are what is left of these great animals. The bones that they left behind have been turned into rock over time. Today scientists can study these great animals by finding the fossils they left behind.

Dinosaur Eggs

Dinosaur eggs have been found all over the world. Some of them are very similar to large ostrich eggs found today. They have been fossilized over time and that is why we can still find them today. They generally tend to have more symmetry and a rounder shape than modern bird eggs. Baby dinosaurs found in fossilized eggs can be studied to learn more about the nature of these wonderful animals.

Dinosaur Egg

Dinosaur Names

The following are common dinosaur names and their meanings. Most names are coined from Greek vocabulary, but some dinosaurs are named after their place where they were discovered.

1. Albertosaurus -"Lizard of Alberta" refers to the fact that it was discovered in
Alberta.

2. Allosaurus -"Strange Lizard" due to its unusual bone structures.

3. Apatosaurus-"Deceptive Lizard" because it had bones similar to another dinosaur's bones. The confusion caused by this fact made the discoverer call the dinosaur deceptive.

4. Baryonyx -"Heavy Claw" because the first fossil to be found was a claw, and because this dinosaur's hands have large claws.

5. Brontosaurus- "Thunder Beast"

6. Coelophysis -"Hollow form"

7. Cynognathus -"Dog jawed" , because it has a jaw like a dog.

8. Deinonychus -"Terrible claw", refers to the large claws on its feet.

9. Dilophosaurus -"Two-crested lizard" because of the protuberances on its head.

10. Dimetrodon -"Two size of teeth" because it has a set of large teeth and a set of small teeth.

11. Dimorphodon- "Two types of teeth" possessed two different types of teeth, which is noteworthy for a reptile.

12. Diplocaulus- "Double stalk."

13. Diplodocus -"Double beamed lizard."

14. Dolichorhynchops -"Long-nosed snout."

15. Dromaesaurus -"Running lizard."

16. Elasmosaurus -"Thin plated lizard."

17. Gallimimus -"Bird mimic" because this dinosaur looks like a bird.

18. Giganotosaurus-"Giant lizard of south" refers to the gigantic size of this dinosaur.

19. Hesperonis- "Regal western bird."

20. Ichthyosaurus -"Fish lizard" because this dinosaur lived in the ocean.

21. Iguanodon -"Iguana tooth" the tooth of this dinosaur resembled that of an iguana.

22. Kronosaurus- "Titan lizard" refers to this dinosaur's large size.

23. Liopleurodon -"Smooth-sided teeth."

24. Maiasaurus -"Good mother lizard."

25. Megalodon -"Big-toothed shark" because this shark has enormous teeth.

26. Mosasaurus- "Meuse lizard."

27. Nothosaurus - "False lizard."

28. Ornitholestes-"Bird robber."

29. Ornithomimus-"Bird mimic" because of its bird-like appearance.

30. Oviraptor- "Egg thief" because they were believed to be taking eggs of other animals.

31. Plesiosaurs -"Close to lizard."

32. Pliosaurs -"More lizards."

33. Protoceratops-"First horn face" because of its single horn.

34. Pteradactyl- "Winged-fingered lizard" because of its long fingers which seemed to form a wing.

35. Pteranodon -"Winged, without teeth" because this dinosaur has a toothless beak and wings.

36. Quetzacoatlus- was named after the Aztec god Quetzalcoatl.

37. Saltopus -"Jumping Foot", because the first fossil found of this dinosaur was a leaping foot.

38. Spinosaurus- "Thorn lizard" because of the paddle-like spines protruding from its back.

39. Stegosaurus- "Roofed lizard" because it had bones on the back.

40. Suchomimus -"Crocodile mimic" because it looks like a crocodile in appearance.

41. Triceratops -"Three-horned face" refers to the three horns protruding from this dinosaurs head.

42. Trilobites- "Three lobes" refers to the tripartite structure of this creature's body.

43. Troodon- "Wounding tooth" refers to the dinosaur's sharp teeth.

44. Tyrannosaurus Rex -"Tyrant lizard" because this dinosaur is terrible to behold.

45. Utahraptor- "Robber from Utah", this dinosaur was named after the
place it was first discovered.

46. Velociraptor- "Speedy robber."

47. Yangchuanosaurus -"Yanchuan Lizard" because it was discovered in Yangchua.

Dinosaur Diet

The diet of an average dinosaur consisted either of plants, meat, insects, or some combination of the above. The dinosaurs which ate plants exclusively are called herbivores which literally means "plant eater." These dinosaurs ate fruit, leaves, grass, and roots from the earth and from trees. These dinosaurs possessed blunt, interlocking teeth which allowed them to easily grind up their vegetable diet. Some of these dinosaurs would eat rocks to help them digest their meals. It is speculated that these dinosaurs ate a lot, drank a lot, and slept a lot.

Other dinosaurs were carnivores which literally means "meat eater." These dinosaurs are more famous than herbivores because they are commonly depicted as the antagonists in dinosaur movies: think Tyrannosaurus Rex. Carnivores would hunt other dinosaurs down and eat them in order to feet. If they were anything like modern day predators, their primary source of food was herbivorous dinosaurs. Carnivores were built for speed and possessed sharp teeth and sharp talons. They would use their speed to catch their prey, their claws to grip the grey, and their teeth to kill their prey. Some of these predators lived in packs and they would hunt together in order to bring down large prey they would otherwise not be able to kill.

Omnivores were dinosaurs which ate meat, insects, and vegetation. Omnivore literally means "all-eater." These dinosaurs would generally eat whatever was commonly available and sometimes they were scavengers. Scavengers eat the remains of animals which were killed by carnivores. These dinosaurs were specially adapted because they could survive in environments where other dinosaurs would die. If an area lacked meat or vegetation, an omnivore would survive but a herbivore or carnivore would die because of lack of food.

Feathered Dinosaurs

Shandong Tianyu Museum's discovery of partial pieces of fossils suggest that certain dinosaurs had feathers. A small skeleton of a dinosaur discovered later proved that the museum was correct. The fossil possessed feathers. Now scientists are speculating that a large variety of dinosaurs possessed feathers and these discoveries back up scientist's claims that some dinosaurs evolved into modern-day birds. Many of these feathered fossils are being discovered in China. These feathered dinosaurs possessed very complex and unique teeth. They were pointed, sharp, and peculiarly large. The teeth in their back jaws were broad and flat. Their teeth seem to indicate that they were able to eat both meat and vegetation, thus making them omnivores.

Plant Eating Dinosaurs

Herbivorous dinosaurs were well adapted to eating plants because of their teeth and long neck. Their teeth were built specially for grinding down plant matter, and some dinosaurs had long necks which allowed them to eat from the tops of trees. The following dinosaurs are common herbivorous dinosaurs.

1. Sauropodomorphs

They are also known as prosauropods. They consist of dinosaurs such as Plateosaurus ,Massopondylus, Lufengosaurus and Anchisaurus. They were able to feed on trees up to a height of 1.2 meters. They had well adapted teeth which were roughened and diamond shaped which allowed for easy tearing of vegetation. They had thick muscles at the gizzards that helped to break down the food.

2. Ornithischains

They had horny peak that was sharp and protruding out of the mouth for cropping plants. Teeth were adapted for tearing the picked plant food before swallowing. They had a fleshy cheek which covered parts of the side of their mouths. In this group there were dinosaurs such as lesothosaurus, Orodromes and the Scelosaurus.

3. Larger ornithopods

They included dinosaurs such as Ouranosaurus, Iguanodonand, Hadrosaurus. They had a beak which was sharp and broad for picking plant foods. They had interlocking teeth which allowed them to tear vegetation easily.

4. Larger ceratopians

They had extremely narrow beak which resembles that of a parrot. The beak was used to feed on vegetation by cutting the vegetation. They had more than one hundred teeth behind the beak; the teeth were interlocking for easy chewing of the plants picked. Psittacosaurus was a ceratopian.

The Weirdest Dinosaurs

Let's discuss a few of the weirdest dinosaurs known to humans.

Oviraptor- This dinosaur looked very similar to a modern day ostrich.
Oviraptor was weird in the sense that it already had bird like features before it became extinct.

Ouranosaurs- They had spines coming out of their backbone which means it had a sail on its back, or a large hump of flesh like a modern day camel. Since it was discovered in a desert, it is possible that it was a camel-like dinosaur.

Carnotaurus- Looked like a tiny Tyrannosaurs Rex. The Carnotaur had horns on its eyebrows and incredibly tiny arms.

Mamenchisaurus was herbivore but what made it weird was the length of its neck. It had an enormous 35-40 foot neck and not
surprisingly, it could never stretch it to full length upwards but had to carry it parallel to the ground.

The Deadliest Dinosaurs

Here are some of the deadliest dinosaurs. These dinosaurs were the lions, tigers, and bears of their time, only much, much larger.

1.Tyrannosaurus Rex
It had numerous strong and sharp teeth. This dinosaur was incredibly large and was probably the apex predator wherever it lived.

2. Utahraptor dinosaur
It had single curved claws which looked like a knife attached to its feet. These dinosaurs might have hunted in packs which made bringing down prey an easier task.

3 Jeholopterus
This dinosaur had sharp fangs. It is believed that the Jeholopterus made a living by sucking blood from other dinosaurs such as large sauropods (long-neck dinosaurs).

4. Kronosaurus
This is believed to have been bigger than the present great white shark. It possessed bigger teeth and a bigger jaw size. Think of a whale-sized shark coming after you.

5. Allosaurus
The Allosaurus was a fierce predator. This is proven by its very powerful jaws and sharp claws.

6. Sarcosuchus

This was the largest crocodile of the dinosaur age. Its length was double that of the largest crocodiles today and its weight was equal to 10 modern-day crocodiles. It had a long and powerful neck which allowed it to jump out of the water with lightning-quick speed.

7. Giganotosaurus

It had a weight of about 8 tons and three strong fingers on each of its hands. It was the largest predator that ever existed on earth. A full grown Gigantosaurus was probably able to bring down full-grown sauropods (long-neck dinosaurs).

Flying Dinosaurs

There are several species of dinosaurs which could fly or glide. Here are four of the flying dinosaurs that inhabited the earth millions of years ago.

Dimorphodon is one of the flying dinosaurs that existed during the age of reptiles. This type of dinosaur had two kinds of teeth and it was around 3.3 feet in length with a wing span of 4 feet. Due to its inability to stand and walk, this dinosaur spent a lot of time perched when not flying.

Dimorphodon

Rhamphorhynchus in another flying dinosaur that had short legs, a long tail that was made of ligaments, and a wing span of 3 feet in length. It had a narrow jaw with very sharp teeth and had a beak which it probably used to catch fish.

Rhamphorhynchus

The *Quetzalcoatlus* was discovered in North America and it is known to be one of the largest flying reptiles during the time dinosaurs were living on earth. Its wing span was 36 feet in length, and it had large eyes, a crested head, a very thin beak and its weight is speculated to have been around 300 pounds. The bones of this flying dinosaur were hollow which meant it could fly for very long distances.

Quetzalcoatlus

The *Pterodactyus* lived near water and its diet consisted of fish and other kinds of small animals. Its wing span was 20 to 30 inches.

Kinds of Dinosaurs

There were many different types of dinosaurs. Here is how scientists have classified them.

Dino Basics

A famous British scientist named Harry Seeley, in 1800's proposed a classification based on their hip structure. Seeley classified two major groups called Ornithischia (bird-hipped) and Saurischia (lizard-hipped). These two types were further broken down into sub groups as follows:

Ornithischia

Thyreophora: Also known as the armored dinosaurs, these dinosaurs were herbivores (plant eaters) and lived in the early Jurassic to the late Creaceous age. Thyrephora simply means "shield bearers" because these type of dinosaurs had armor, plates and horns. This group included Stegosaurus, Ankylosaurusand Nodosauus.

Ornithischia

Cerapods: These are typically horned or duck-billed dinosaurs Just like the Thyreophora, Cerapods were herbivores however, these dinosaurs has better teeth that helped them grind plants better. Cerapods were able to extract more nutrients from their food because of their more advanced jaws.

Saurischia
Theropods: The name means "beast feet." Typically, these dinosaurs moved on two legs and were carnivores (meat eaters). Some of these kinds of dinosaurs were also omnivores (ate both plants and meat). Theropods lived from the late Triassic period until the end of Cretaceous period. Scientists have also discovered that birds are the evolved-descendants of Theropods. While the scary looking and most popular ones in this category are the Tyrannosaurus Rex and Veliociraptor, there were also other dinosaurs like Spinosaurus, Deinonychus, Allosaurus, Carnotaurus,

Albertosaurus, Megalosaurus, Yangchuanosaurus and much more.

Sauropods: These lizard-footed type of dinosaurs walked on four legs and were enormous in size. They had long necks and tails, were huge in size and had comparatively small heads. Sauropods were herbivores and included Brachiosaurus, Diplodocus, Seismosaurus, Giraffatitan, and Apatosaurus.

The Biggest Dinosaurs

During the Jurassic period there were many heavy, gigantic dinosaurs that roamed all throughout the earth. Some of the biggest dinosaurs are listed below:

Liopleurodon - Liopleurodon looked similar to an orca and a shark, and it was the biggest pliosaur. It had a massive body, huge flippers, and a long thick jaw full of teeth. Palaeontologists say that this type of dinosaur weighed over 30 tons and could grow to a length of 50 feet.

Quetzalcoatlus - This type of dinosaur was also huge in size as it had a wingspan of 45 feet. This huge pterosaur has received its name from the winged Aztec god.

Spinosaurus - Spinosaurus was heavier than Tyrannosaurus Rex and it is believed that they were bigger in size too. It had a mouth that was similar to crocodile's mouth and it also had a skin flap that protruded from its back which resembled a sail. It is believed that the sail helped the dinosaur regulate its body temperature.

Argentinosaurus - As the name suggests, the fossils of this dinosaur was found in Argentina. It was among the biggest dinosaurs with weight of over 100 tons and height of up to 120 feet. A single spinal vertebra is four feet in diameter.

Argentinosaurus

The Smallest Dinosaurs

Fossils have helped palaeontologists discover the smallest dinosaurs that lived on earth. They are as follows: The Humming Bird - It may seem strange, but palaeontologists believe that dinosaurs did not become extinct completely but underwent evolution. Humming birds are believed to be the evolutionary descendants of dinosaurs that lived millions of years ago. It weighs as little as one-tenth of an ounce, and is considered to be the smallest dinosaur species that lives today.

Lariosaurus - With a total weight of about 20 pounds and a length of 2 feet, this dinosaur was the smallest aquatic dinosaur. It had a long pointed tail and a streamlined body. It usually lived in water but it also dwelt on land. It was similar to amphibians because it could live in both environments.

Pterosaurus - Pterosaurus had hollow bones and were lightly built. The pterosaurs were of different sizes but the smallest one was just a few inches long. This carnivorous dinosaur ate insects, crabs and fishes.

Microceratops - The microceratops was the smallest herbivorous dinosaur. It weighed 4 pounds and had a height of about a foot and a half.

Microaptor - The microaptors were the smallest carnivorous dinosaurs. They had a height of just 2 feet from head to tail. They were also known as "four-winged dinosaur" because they had feathers on their legs and arms. Their diet consisted only of insects.

Author Bio

Enrique Fiesta

I was born in Southwest Florida and I hold a degree in Latin and Greek language and literature. In addition to my principal studies, I have also studied philosophy, history, the natural sciences, and literature. In my spare time I devote the vast majority of my time to reading, writing, praying, and walking. I am currently pursuing legal studies in order to become an attorney. After I earn my law degree I intend to pursue a doctorate in philosophy, literature, and politics.

Our books are available at
1. Amazon.com
2. Barnes and Noble
3. Itunes
4. Kobo
5. Smashwords
6. Google Play Books

Publisher

JD-Biz Corp

P O Box 374

Mendon, Utah 84325

http://www.jd-biz.com/

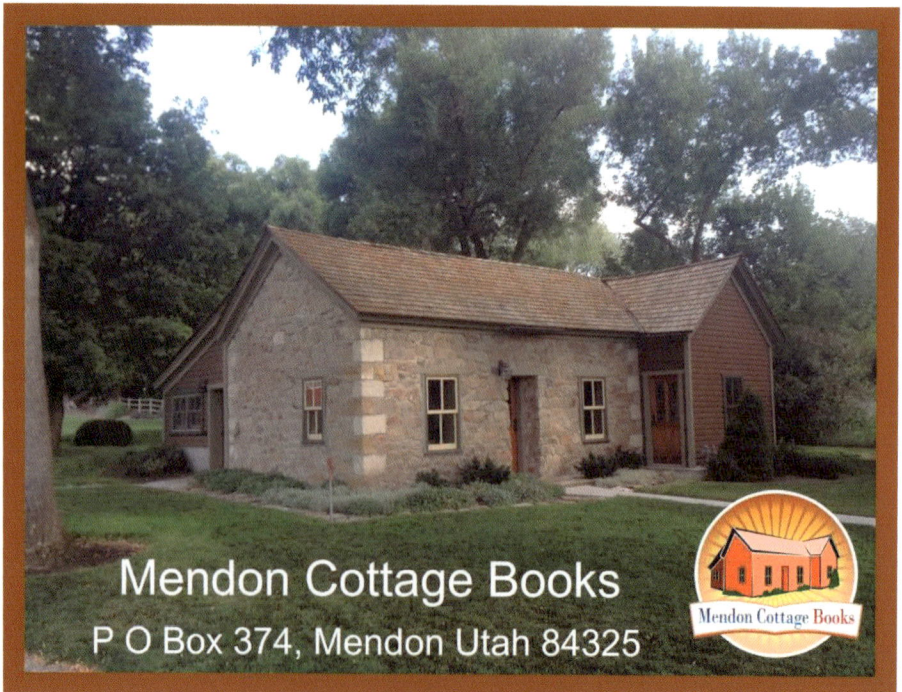

Mendon Cottage Books

P O Box 374, Mendon Utah 84325

Top Ten Dog Breeds
For Kids

Amazing Animal Books
For Young Readers
Kisha Bennett & John Davidson

Poodles
Dog Books for Kids
K. Bennett

Labrador Retrievers
Dog Books for Kids
K. Bennett

German Shepherds
Dog Books for Kids
K. Bennett

Rottweilers
Dog Books for Kids
K. Bennett

Boxers
Dog Books for Kids
K. Bennett

Golden Retrievers
Dog Books for Kids
K. Bennett

Beagles
Dog Books for Kids
K. Bennett

Yorkies
Dog Books for Kids
K. Bennett

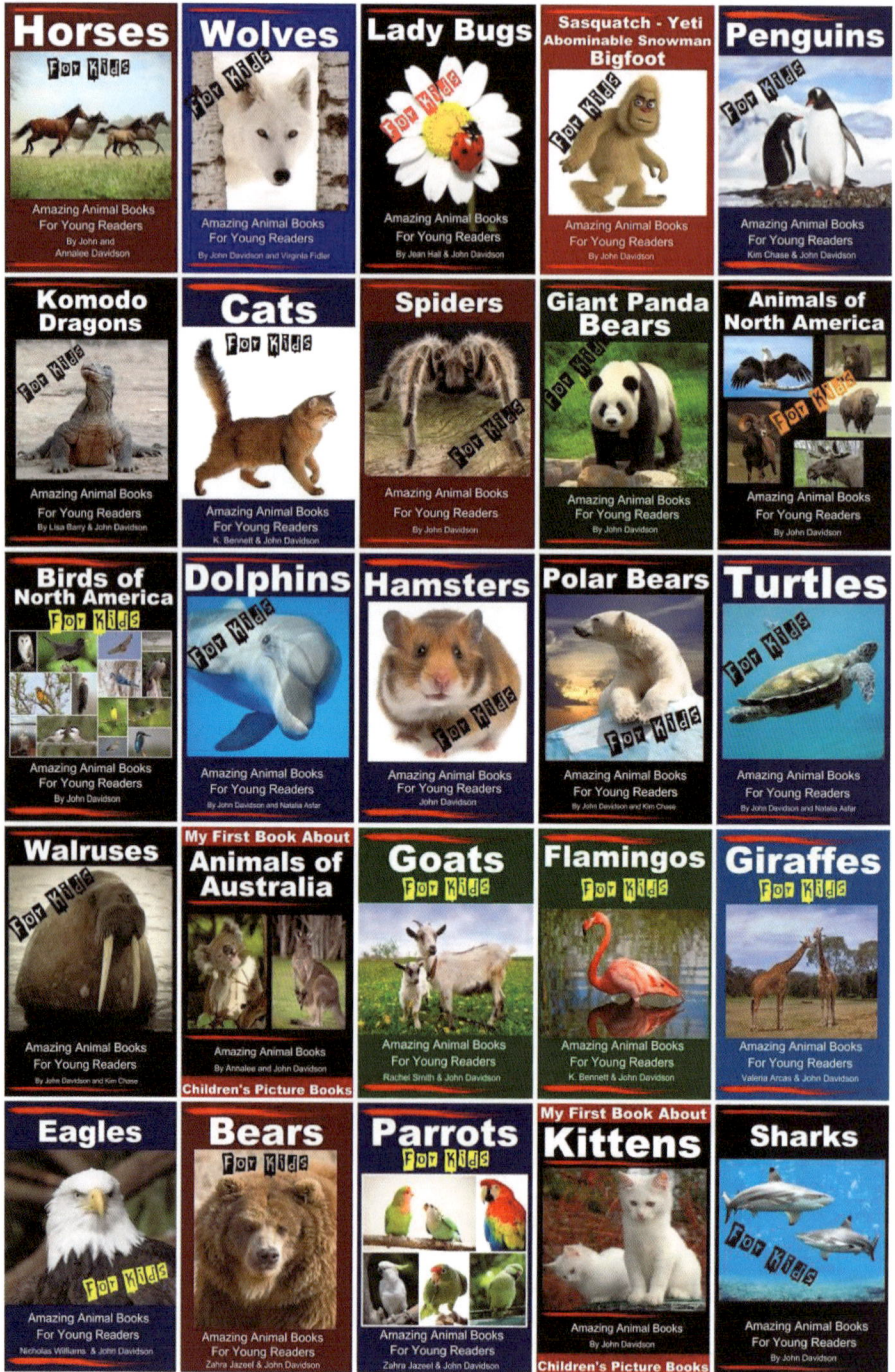

Horses — For Kids — Amazing Animal Books For Young Readers — By John and Annalee Davidson

Wolves — For Kids — Amazing Animal Books For Young Readers — By John Davidson and Virginia Fidler

Lady Bugs — For Kids — Amazing Animal Books For Young Readers — By Jean Hall & John Davidson

Sasquatch - Yeti Abominable Snowman Bigfoot — For Kids — Amazing Animal Books For Young Readers — By John Davidson

Penguins — For Kids — Amazing Animal Books For Young Readers — Kim Chase & John Davidson

Komodo Dragons — For Kids — Amazing Animal Books For Young Readers — By Lisa Barry & John Davidson

Cats — For Kids — Amazing Animal Books For Young Readers — K. Bennett & John Davidson

Spiders — For Kids — Amazing Animal Books For Young Readers — By John Davidson

Giant Panda Bears — For Kids — Amazing Animal Books For Young Readers — By John Davidson

Animals of North America — For Kids — Amazing Animal Books For Young Readers — By John Davidson

Birds of North America — For Kids — Amazing Animal Books For Young Readers — By John Davidson

Dolphins — For Kids — Amazing Animal Books For Young Readers — By John Davidson and Natalia Asfar

Hamsters — For Kids — Amazing Animal Books For Young Readers — John Davidson

Polar Bears — For Kids — Amazing Animal Books For Young Readers — By John Davidson and Kim Chase

Turtles — For Kids — Amazing Animal Books For Young Readers — By John Davidson and Natalia Asfar

Walruses — For Kids — Amazing Animal Books For Young Readers — By John Davidson and Kim Chase

My First Book About Animals of Australia — Amazing Animal Books — By Annalee and John Davidson — Children's Picture Books

Goats — For Kids — Amazing Animal Books For Young Readers — Rachel Smith & John Davidson

Flamingos — For Kids — Amazing Animal Books For Young Readers — K. Bennett & John Davidson

Giraffes — For Kids — Amazing Animal Books For Young Readers — Valeria Arcas & John Davidson

Eagles — For Kids — Amazing Animal Books For Young Readers — Nicholas Williams & John Davidson

Bears — For Kids — Amazing Animal Books For Young Readers — Zahra Jazeel & John Davidson

Parrots — For Kids — Amazing Animal Books For Young Readers — Zahra Jazeel & John Davidson

My First Book About Kittens — Amazing Animal Books — By John Davidson — Children's Picture Books

Sharks — For Kids — Amazing Animal Books For Young Readers — By John Davidson

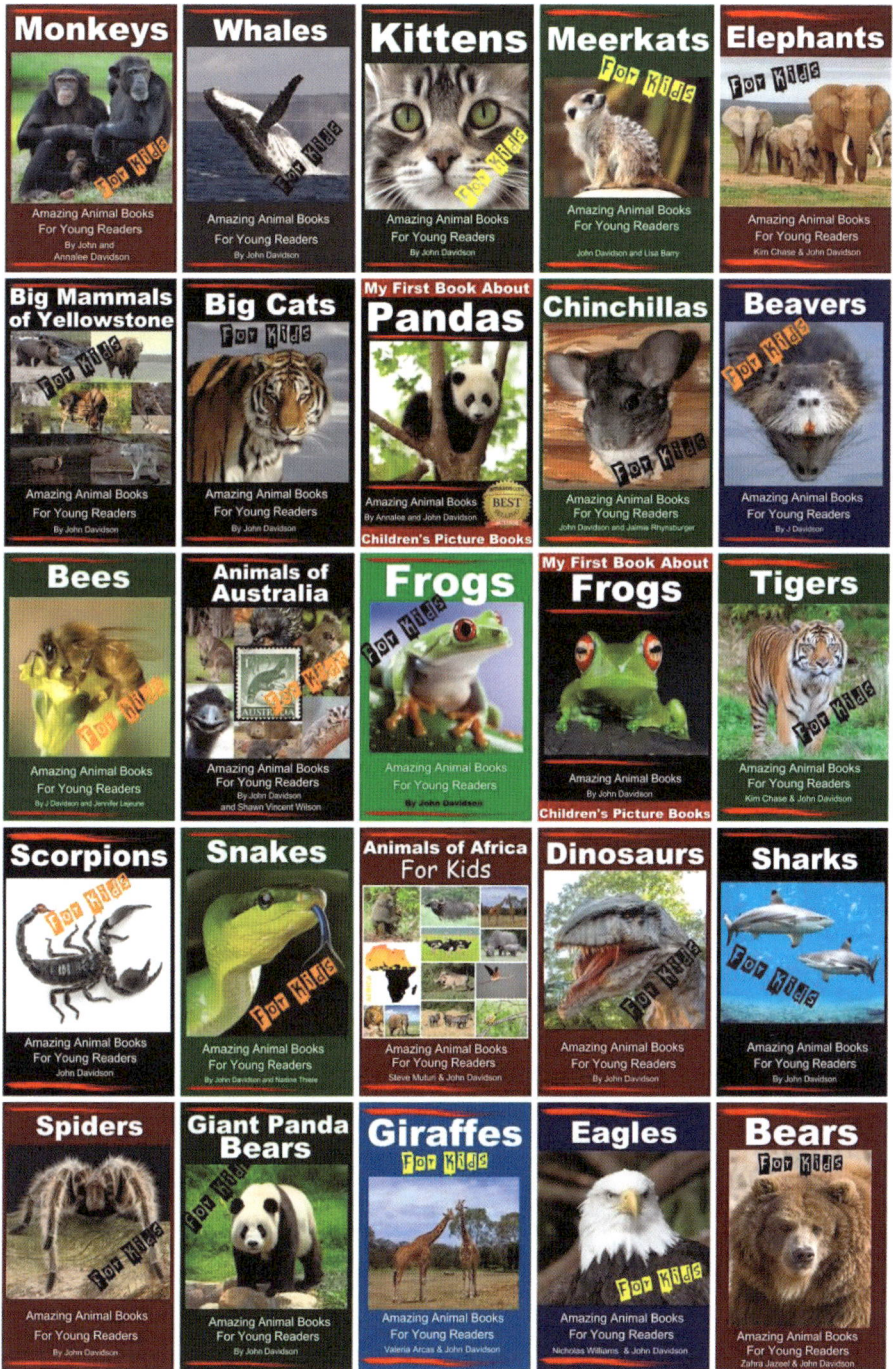

Monkeys

Amazing Animal Books
For Young Readers
By John and
Annalee Davidson

Whales

Amazing Animal Books
For Young Readers
By John Davidson

Kittens

Amazing Animal Books
For Young Readers
By John Davidson

Meerkats
For Kids

Amazing Animal Books
For Young Readers
John Davidson and Lisa Barry

Elephants
For Kids

Amazing Animal Books
For Young Readers
Kim Chase & John Davidson

Big Mammals of Yellowstone

Amazing Animal Books
For Young Readers
By John Davidson

Big Cats
For Kids

Amazing Animal Books
For Young Readers
By John Davidson

My First Book About
Pandas

Amazing Animal Books
By Annalee and John Davidson
Children's Picture Books

Chinchillas

Amazing Animal Books
For Young Readers
John Davidson and Jaimie Rhymsburger

Beavers
For Kids

Amazing Animal Books
For Young Readers
By J Davidson

Bees

Amazing Animal Books
For Young Readers
By J Davidson and Jennifer Lejeune

Animals of Australia

Amazing Animal Books
For Young Readers
By John Davidson
and Shawn Vincent Wilson

Frogs
For Kids

Amazing Animal Books
For Young Readers
By John Davidson

My First Book About
Frogs

Amazing Animal Books
By John Davidson
Children's Picture Books

Tigers

Amazing Animal Books
For Young Readers
Kim Chase & John Davidson

Scorpions
For Kids

Amazing Animal Books
For Young Readers
John Davidson

Snakes
For Kids

Amazing Animal Books
For Young Readers
By John Davidson and Nadine Thiele

Animals of Africa
For Kids

Amazing Animal Books
For Young Readers
Steve Muturi & John Davidson

Dinosaurs
For Kids

Amazing Animal Books
For Young Readers
By John Davidson

Sharks
For Kids

Amazing Animal Books
For Young Readers
By John Davidson

Spiders
For Kids

Amazing Animal Books
For Young Readers
By John Davidson

Giant Panda Bears
For Kids

Amazing Animal Books
For Young Readers
By John Davidson

Giraffes
For Kids

Amazing Animal Books
For Young Readers
Valeria Arcas & John Davidson

Eagles
For Kids

Amazing Animal Books
For Young Readers
Nicholas Williams & John Davidson

Bears
For Kids

Amazing Animal Books
For Young Readers
Zahra Jazeel & John Davidson

Printed in Great Britain
by Amazon